Level 4 Diploma in Accounting
Personal Tax
Finance Act 2011

GW00514829

Third edition July 2011

ISBN 9781 4453 7875 6
(Previous ISBN 9780 7517 8681 1)

British Library Cataloguing-in-Publication Data

A catalogue record for this book is available from the British Library

Published by

BPP Learning Media Ltd, BPP House, Aldine Place, London W12 8AA

www.bpp.com/learningmedia

Printed in the United Kingdom

Your learning materials, published by BPP Learning Media Ltd,
are printed on paper sourced from sustainable, managed forests.

All our rights reserved. No part of this publication may be reproduced, stored in a retrieval
system or transmitted, in any form or by any means, electronic, mechanical, photocopying,
recording or otherwise, without the prior written permission of BPP Learning Media Ltd.

©
BPP Learning Media Ltd
2011

Welcome to BPP Learning Media's AAT **Passcards for Personal Tax.**

- They **save you time**. Important topics are summarised for you.

- They incorporate **diagrams** to kick start your memory.

- They follow the overall **structure** of the BPP Text, but BPP Learning Media's AAT **Passcards** are not just a condensed book. Each card has been separately designed for clear presentation. Topics are self contained and can be grasped visually.

- AAT **Passcards** are still **just the right size** for pockets, briefcases and bags.

- AAT **Passcards focus on the essential points you need to know in the workplace, or when taking your assessment.**

Run through the complete set of **Passcards** as often as you can in the weeks leading up to your assessment. The day before the assessment, try to go through the **Passcards** again! You will then be well on your way to assessment success.

Good luck!

Contents

The BPP Learning Media **Question Bank** contains tasks and assessments that provide invaluable practice in the skills you need to complete this assessment successfully.

1: The tax framework

Topic List

Tax on individuals

Tax law and guidance

Tax practitioners

Confidentiality

In this background chapter we deal with the administration of UK tax and the ethical consideration for tax practitioners.

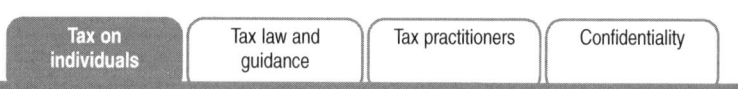

| Tax on individuals | Tax law and guidance | Tax practitioners | Confidentiality |

Tax on individuals

Liability to tax

- Income tax
- Capital gains

For tax year
eg. 6/04/11 to 5/04/12
(2011/12)

HMRC

Administers UK tax

Records

- Employment income: Salary, benefits
- Property income: Tenancy agreements invoices of receipts/expenses
- Savings income: Interest statement
- Dividend income: Dividend certificates
- General: Gift Aid, pension contributions

For 2011/12
retain until 31/01/14
unless has
property/trading income,
then need to retain **all**
records until 31/01/18.

Tax law

- Statute Law: Acts of Parliament
- Case Law

■ Detailed regulations in Statutory Instruments (SIs).

Does not have force of law. ■

HMRC Guidance

- Statements of practice
- Extra statutory concessions
- Leaflets
- Revenue and Customs Briefs
- Manuals
- Working Together

Tax on individuals | Tax law and guidance | **Tax practitioners** | Confidentiality

Guidelines on Professional Ethics
- Integrity
- Objectivity
- Professional competence and due care
- Confidentiality
- Professional behaviour

Responsibilities
- to clients
- to HMRC

Money laundering
- Conversion of criminal proceeds into assets that appear to have non-criminal origin
- Report to Money Laundering Reporting Officer (firm) or SOCA (sole practitioner)

Omission/error in tax return
- Notify client that cannot act further
- Make money laundering report

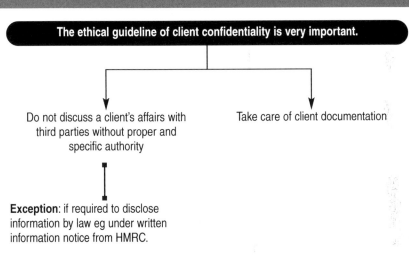

The ethical guideline of client confidentiality is very important.

Do not discuss a client's affairs with third parties without proper and specific authority

Take care of client documentation

Exception: if required to disclose information by law eg under written information notice from HMRC.

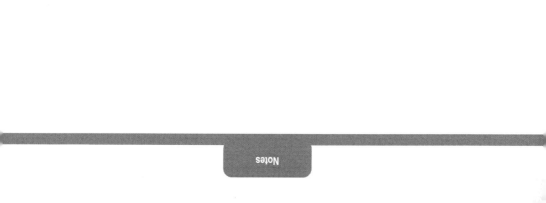

Notes

2: Employment income

Topic List

Employment and self-employment

Employment income

Taxable benefits

Exempt benefits

Allowable deductions

You must be able to identify if an individual is employed or self-employed because there are different tax rules applicable.

There are also allowable deductions that can be taken into account when computing employment income. It is important that you can calculate an employee's earnings. This will include the taxable value of any benefits provided by reason of the employment.

You may also be required to complete a supplementary employment page that accompanies the income tax return form.

Employment and self-employment

An employee works under a contract of service and a self-employed person under a contract for services.

Factors that may be of importance in deciding whether a person is employed or self-employed:

- the degree of control exercised over the person doing the work
- whether person must be offered and accept further work
- whether he provides his own equipment
- whether he hires his own helpers
- what degree of financial risk he takes
- what degree of responsibility for investment and management he has
- whether he can profit from sound management
- whether he can work when he chooses
- whether he is entitled to holiday and sickness pay
- wording used in agreement

Employment income

Employees/directors are taxed on income from the employment:

- Cash earnings
- Benefits

■ Salaries, wages, bonuses, commissions, fees and tips.

Earnings are taxed in the year in which they are received.

The general definition of the date of receipt is the earlier of:

- The time payment is made
- The time entitlement to payment arises

Directors are deemed to receive earnings on the earliest of the following:

- The time given by the above general rule
- The time the amount is credited in the company's accounting records
- The end of the company's period of account (if the amount has been determined by then)
- When the amount is determined (if this is after the end of the company's period of account)

Company car

The annual taxable benefit for the private use of a car is (price of car − capital contributions*) × %.

- The % depends on the level of the car's CO_2 emissions.
- The benefit is scaled down on a time available basis. The benefit is then reduced by any contribution by the employee for private use.
- Fuel for private use is charged at £18,800 × CO_2 %, with no reduction for partial reimbursement by the employee.

* Maximum of £5,000 capital contribution can be deducted

Vans

- £3,000 benefit if available for private use (does not include home to work travel)
- £550 private fuel benefit

Loans

① Loans of over £5,000 (aggregate) give rise to taxable benefits equal to the difference between the actual interest and interest at the official rate.

② A write-off of a loan gives rise to a taxable benefit equal to the amount written off.

Accommodation

Basic charge: higher of annual value and rent paid by employer

Additional charge if cost more than £75,000: (cost − £75k) × interest %

No charge on job related accommodation

If acquired more than 6 years before first provided to employee, MV when first provided.

Living expenses

Living expenses connected with accommodation (eg gas bills) are taxable. However, if the accommodation is job-related, the maximum amount taxable is 10% of net earnings.

Vouchers

Cash vouchers - cash value

Other vouchers - cost to employer

Private use of asset

In general, if an asset is made available for private use, the annual taxable benefit is 20% of the market value when the asset was first provided, less any employee contribution.

If the asset is subsequently given to the employee the taxable benefit is the higher of:

(i) Market value at date first provided, less amounts already taxed
(ii) Market value at date of gift

Less any employee contribution.

Example

Sue was lent a TV by her employer on 6 July 2011. The market value of the TV was then £800. Sue uses the TV for private purposes.

The taxable benefit in 2011/12 is

$$£800 \times 20\% \times {}^{9}/_{12} = £120$$

Note. As the TV was not available for the entire year the benefit is pro-rated.

Exempt benefits

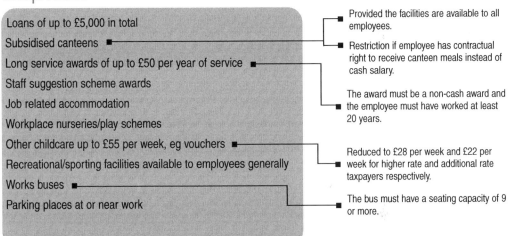

Loans of up to £5,000 in total

Subsidised canteens ▪ ──────────── Provided the facilities are available to all employees.

────── Restriction if employee has contractual right to receive canteen meals instead of cash salary.

Long service awards of up to £50 per year of service ▪

Staff suggestion scheme awards

Job related accommodation

Workplace nurseries/play schemes

───── The award must be a non-cash award and the employee must have worked at least 20 years.

Other childcare up to £55 per week, eg vouchers ▪

Recreational/sporting facilities available to employees generally

───── Reduced to £28 per week and £22 per week for higher rate and additional rate taxpayers respectively.

Works buses ▪ ──────────────

Parking places at or near work

───── The bus must have a seating capacity of 9 or more.

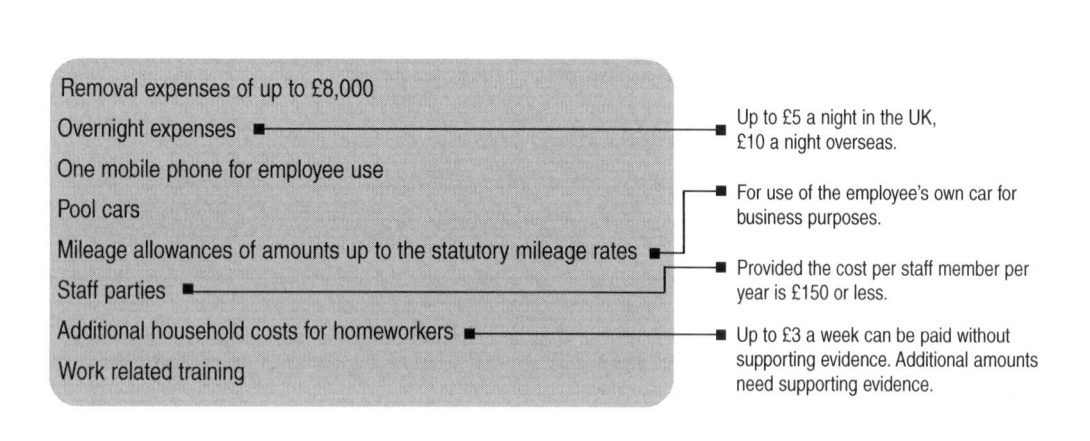

Removal expenses of up to £8,000

Overnight expenses ■————————————— ■ Up to £5 a night in the UK, £10 a night overseas.

One mobile phone for employee use

Pool cars

Mileage allowances of amounts up to the statutory mileage rates ■————— ■ For use of the employee's own car for business purposes.

Staff parties ■————————————— ■ Provided the cost per staff member per year is £150 or less.

Additional household costs for homeworkers ■————— ■ Up to £3 a week can be paid without supporting evidence. Additional amounts need supporting evidence.

Work related training

The general rule is that expenses can only be deducted from earnings if they are incurred wholly, exclusively and necessarily in performing the duties of the employment.

■ Applied quite strictly.

Expenses specifically deductible against earnings:

(1) **Subscriptions** to relevant professional bodies

(2) **Qualifying travel expenses** – costs the employee incurs travelling in the performance of his duties or/and travelling to or from a place attended in the performance of duties ■

(3) **Contributions** (within limits) to a registered occupational pension scheme

(4) **Payments to charity** under a payroll deduction scheme

Assessment focus

If you have to decide whether an expense is deductible, put yourself in HMRC's position and try to find an argument against deducting it. If you can find a specific argument, the expense is probably not deductible.

■ Normal commuting does not qualify.

■ Relief is available for expenses incurred by an employee working at a temporary location on a secondment of 24 months or less.

An **occupational pension scheme** is a pension scheme provided by an employer registered with HMRC.

> **An employee can deduct contributions made to an occupational pension scheme from his earnings.**

■ Net pay arrangements.

Tax advantages

- Employee contributions are deducted from taxable earnings
- Employer contributions are not a taxable benefit

Contributions

Tax relief on higher of:
- Earnings
- £3,600

Personal pensions

Individuals can set up personal pensions with financial providers eg a bank. Tax relief is dealt with in Chapter 5.

3: Property income

Topic List

Property income

Qualifying holiday accommodation

Rent-a-room

In your assessment you may be required to produce a calculation of property income and to complete the land and property pages on the income tax return form.

You are also expected to understand the special rules relating to qualifying holiday accommodation and the rent-a-room scheme.

Property income covers rent from letting property.

Computation

Calculate property income on an **accruals** basis.

Accounts are drawn up with a year end of 5 April.

Allowable expenses are revenue expenses incurred wholly and exclusively for letting. Capital expenses are not allowable.

Rents and expenses of all properties are pooled to give a single income/loss figure.

- **Exception:**
  For furnished lettings, a 10% wear and tear allowance or the renewals basis can be claimed.

- **Exception:**
  Keep a separate pool of profits/losses from letting qualifying holiday accommodation.

Losses are carried forward against future property income.

Qualifying holiday accommodation

Situated in UK or EEA
Furnished
Let on commercial basis
Available for letting at least 140 days per tax year and let for 70 days
Not more than 155 days of letting to same occupier for more than 31 consecutive days

■ Also called furnished holiday lettings.

① Losses kept separate and relief given against future profits from the same furnished holiday lettings business

② Earnings for pension purposes

③ Capital allowances for furniture

Rent-a-room relief

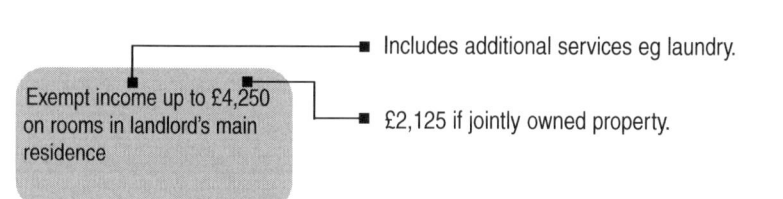

Exempt income up to £4,250 on rooms in landlord's main residence

- Includes additional services eg laundry.

- £2,125 if jointly owned property.

Elections

(by 31/01/14 for 2011/12)

- Ignore rent-a-room (eg if loss)
- Use rent-a-room if income exceeds limit: taxed on income less limit, with no expense relief

4: Taxable income

This chapter identifies the key points you must remember in calculating an individual's taxable income.

Income from all sources is added together in a personal tax computation (total income).

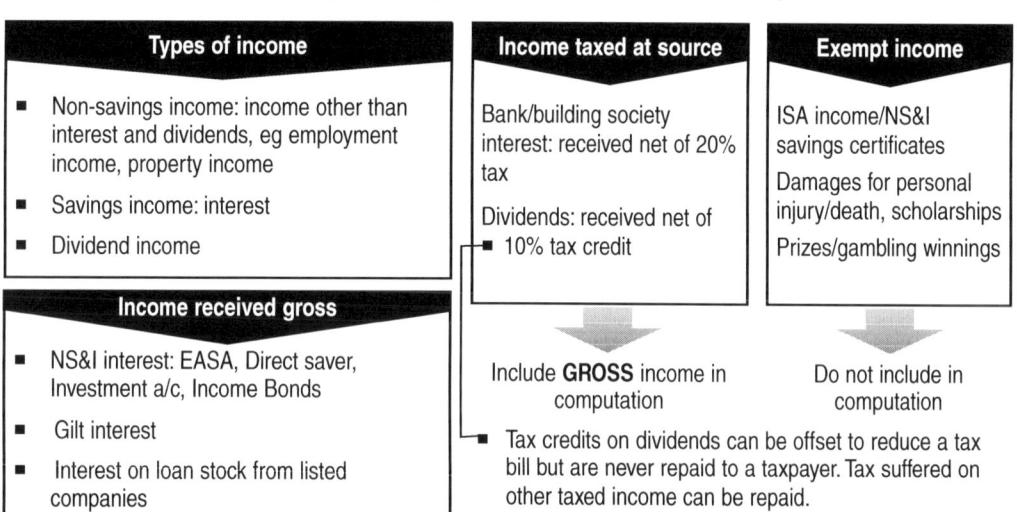

Types of income	Income taxed at source	Exempt income
■ Non-savings income: income other than interest and dividends, eg employment income, property income ■ Savings income: interest ■ Dividend income	Bank/building society interest: received net of 20% tax Dividends: received net of 10% tax credit	ISA income/NS&I savings certificates Damages for personal injury/death, scholarships Prizes/gambling winnings

Income received gross

- NS&I interest: EASA, Direct saver, Investment a/c, Income Bonds
- Gilt interest
- Interest on loan stock from listed companies

Include **GROSS** income in computation

Tax credits on dividends can be offset to reduce a tax bill but are never repaid to a taxpayer. Tax suffered on other taxed income can be repaid.

Do not include in computation

Total income minus the personal allowance or age allowance is taxable income

Personal allowance

1. Personal allowance £7,475 (2011/12)

2. Taxpayers up to age 65 are entitled to a personal allowance

3. Reduced by £1 for every £2 of total income in excess of £100,000, Nil if income is ≥ £114,950

Age allowance

1. Age 65–74, £9,940 (2011/12) Age 75+, £10,090 (2011/12)

2. Age at end of tax year

3. Reduced by £1 for every £2 of total income in excess of £24,000, minimum £7,475 (2011/12)

Income adjusted for Gift Aid and personal pension contributions

Notes

5: Calculation of income tax

In your assessment, you will be expected to compute an individual's income tax liability. This chapter is therefore vitally important.

Topic List

Tax computation

Layout

1. Total non-savings, savings and dividend income separately.
2. Deduct the personal or age allowance first from non-savings, then from savings and then from dividend income.

Savings income starting rate only applies if non-savings income does not exceed £2,560 (2011/12).

Extending basic rate band

The basic rate band is extended by the **GROSS** amount of any Gift Aid donations or any personal pension contributions.

Taxing income

- Non-savings income is taxed first, then savings income, then dividend income is taxed last.

- Non-savings income is taxed at 20% (basic rate), then 40% (higher rate), then 50% (additional rate).

- Savings income is taxed at 10% (savings income starting rate), then 20% (basic rate), then 40% (higher rate), then 50% (additional rate).

- Dividend income within the basic rate tax band is taxed at 10% (not 20%), then 32.5% (higher rate), then 42.5% (additional rate).

These payments are made net of 20% tax.
Extending the basic rate band gives further relief.

6: Self assessment of income tax

Topic List

Returns and records

Penalties

Payment of tax

Interest and late payment of tax

Enquiries

This chapter looks at when returns must be filed and at due dates for the payment of tax. In your assessment you may well be expected to draft a letter to a client advising of these dates.

Filing date

The **filing due date** for filing a tax return online is:

(1) 31 January following the end of the tax year that the return covers,

or

(2) 3 months after the notice to file a return was issued if issued after 31 October following the end of the tax year.

If an individual wishes to file a paper return, the filing date is 31 October following the tax year.

Records

Records must, in general, be kept until the later of:

(1) 5 years after the 31 January following the tax year concerned (where the taxpayer is in business or has property income); or

(2) 1 year after the 31 January following the tax year, otherwise.

Penalties for error

Imposed if inaccurate return for:

- carelessness
- deliberate error but no arrangements to conceal
- deliberate error and arrangements to conceal

Amount of penalty

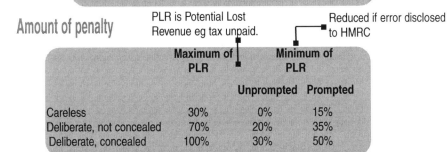

PLR is Potential Lost Revenue eg tax unpaid.

Reduced if error disclosed to HMRC

	Maximum of PLR	Minimum of PLR	
		Unprompted	Prompted
Careless	30%	0%	15%
Deliberate, not concealed	70%	20%	35%
Deliberate, concealed	100%	30%	50%

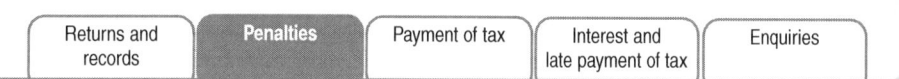

Penalties for late notification

Imposed if does not notify chargeability by 5 October following end of tax year

Amount of penalty

	Maximum of PLR	Minimum of PLR	
		Unprompted	Prompted
Careless	30%	>12m <12m 10% 0%	>12m <12m 20% 10%
Deliberate but not concealed	70%	20%	35%
Deliberate and concealed	100%	30%	50%

Penalties for late filing

- Immediate £100 penalty
- Over 3 months late: £10 per day (max 90 days)
- Between 6 and 12 months late: 5% of tax due
- Over 12 months late:
  - 100% of tax due if deliberate and concealed
  - 70% of tax due if deliberate but not concealed
  - 5% of tax due, otherwise (eg careless)
    min £300 for tax-geared penalties

Penalties for failure to keep records

£3,000 for each failure

6: Self assessment of income tax

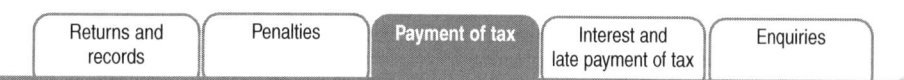

Payment of tax

Payments on account (POA) of income tax must be made on 31 January in tax year and on the following 31 July.

The final payment of income tax must be paid on 31 January following the tax year.

All CGT is due on 31 January following the tax year.

Payments on account

1 Each POA is 50% of the prior tax year's income tax liability less tax suffered at source

2 POAs are not required if the relevant amount falls below £1,000 or > 80% deducted at source

3 A claim may be made to reduce POAs to a stated amount, or nil

Penalties for late payment

Penalties are levied on a final payment of income tax or CGT.

Paid	Penalty
(1) Within 30 days of due date	none
(2) Not more than 6 months after due date	5% of tax due
(3) More than 6 months but less than 12 months from due date	further 5% of tax due
(4) More than 12 months from due date	further 5% of tax due

Penalties are **not** due on payments on account.

Interest

Interest runs on:

(1) POAs from the normal due dates (31 Jan and 31 July).

(2) Any final payment and CGT from the normal due date until the day before payment is actually made.

Enquiries

HMRC may enquire into a return provided they give notice by a year after the receipt of the return if the return is filed on or before the filing due date.

■ if return filed late deadline is one year from 31 Jan, 30 April, 31 July, 31 Oct following actual filing date.

■ HMRC randomly select returns to enquire into. They also select returns where there is an identified tax risk.

7: Computing capital gains tax

Topic List

It is important that you can calculate CGT payable by individuals.

In your assessment, you are likely to be required to compute both chargeable gains and CGT. There are also some special rules that you need to know about such as dealing with part disposals, disposals to connected persons and disposals between spouses/civil partners.

Chargeable persons, disposals and assets

Three elements are needed for a chargeable gain to arise.

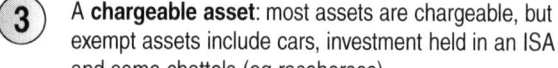

(1) A **chargeable disposal**: this includes sales, gifts and the destruction of assets.

(2) A **chargeable person**: individuals.

(3) A **chargeable asset**: most assets are chargeable, but exempt assets include cars, investment held in an ISA and some chattels (eg racehorses).

| Chargeable persons, disposals and assets | Basic computations | Part disposals | The charge to CGT | Losses | Connected persons | Spouses/Civil partners |

Computation

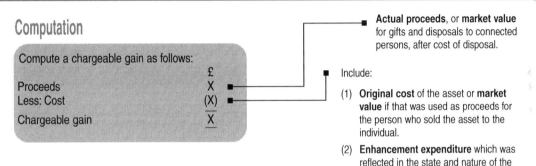

Compute a chargeable gain as follows:

	£
Proceeds	X
Less: Cost	(X)
Chargeable gain	X

- **Actual proceeds**, or **market value** for gifts and disposals to connected persons, after cost of disposal.

- Include:

  (1) **Original cost** of the asset or **market value** if that was used as proceeds for the person who sold the asset to the individual.

  (2) **Enhancement expenditure** which was reflected in the state and nature of the asset at the time of disposal.

  (3) **Incidental costs** of **acquisition**.

Part disposals

On a part disposal, you are only allowed to take part of the cost of the asset into account.

- Costs attributable solely to the part disposed of are taken into account in full
- For other costs, take into account A/(A+B) of the cost
  - A is the proceeds of the part sold
  - B is the market value of the part retained

Example

Mr X owns land that originally cost £30,000. He sold a quarter interest in the land for £18,000. The incidental costs of disposal were £1,000. The market value of the three-quarter share remaining is estimated to be £36,000. What is the chargeable gain?

	£
Proceeds	18,000
Less: Incidental costs of disposal	(1,000)
Less: $30,000 \times \dfrac{18,000}{18,000 + 36,000}$	(10,000)
Chargeable gain	7,000

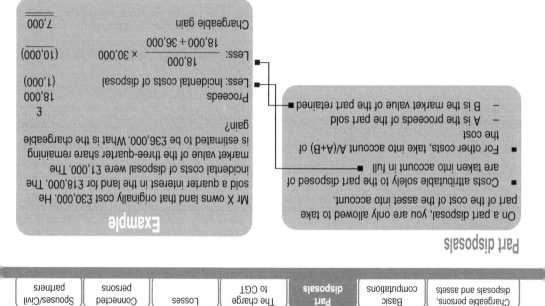

Deduct the CGT annual exempt amount of £10,600 (2011/12) when computing an individual's total taxable gains.

Rate

– 28% if higher or additional rate taxpayer

– 18% on taxable gains up to the amount of the unused basic rate band and 28% on the excess

Due date

CGT for 2011/12 is due on 31 January 2013

Example

Sue made taxable gains (after the annual exempt amount) in July 2011 of £10,000.

She has £6,000 of unused basic rate band.

What CGT must Sue pay?

She must pay CGT of £6,000 × 18% + £4,000 × 28% = £2,200

7: Computing capital gains tax

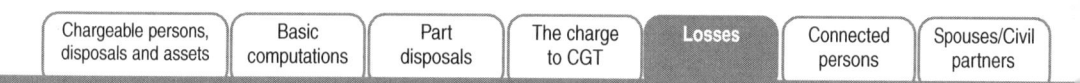

| Chargeable persons, disposals and assets | Basic computations | Part disposals | The charge to CGT | Losses | Connected persons | Spouses/Civil partners |

Deduct allowable capital losses from chargeable gains in the tax year in which they arise.

Any loss which cannot be set off is carried forward to set against future chargeable gains.

Allowable losses brought forward are only set off to reduce current year chargeable gains less current year allowable losses to the annual exempt amount.

Example

Zoë made net chargeable gains of £13,600 in 2011/12. She had brought forward capital losses of £8,000.

Brought forward capital losses of £3,000 will be set off in 2011/12. The remaining losses of £5,000 will be carried forward to 2012/13.

Connected persons

Disposals between connected persons are deemed to be at the market values of the assets. If a loss arises on a disposal to a connected person it can only be set against future chargeable gains on disposals to the **same** connected person.

An individual is connected with his spouse/civil partner and with his and his spouse's/civil partner's relatives (brothers, sisters, ancestors and lineal descendants) and their spouses/civil partners.

- **Exception**: Does not apply to no gain/no loss disposals (eg to spouse/civil partner).

Spouses/civil partners

- Disposals between spouses/civil partners do not give rise to gains or losses.
- The acquiring spouse/civil partner is treated as acquiring the asset for proceeds equal to the disposing spouse/civil partner's base cost.

Example

Gavin gifted an asset to his civil partner, Greg. The asset had originally cost Gavin £10,000, but it was worth £17,000 at the time of the gift.

Deemed proceeds	£10,000
Less: cost	(£10,000)
	no gain/no loss

* Base cost to Greg for future disposals = £10,000

8: Chattels and private residences

Topic List

In this chapter we look at the rules that apply for calculating taxable gains on chattels and private residences.

Chattels

A chattel is an item of **tangible moveable property** (eg a painting).

Remaining useful life of 50 years or less (eg racehorse)

Gains on chattels sold for gross proceeds of £6,000 or less and on wasting chattels are **exempt**.

The maximum gain on chattels sold for mor
is **5/3 (gross proceeds − £6,000)**.

Losses on chattels sold for under £6,000 are restricted by **assuming the gross proceeds to be £6,000**.

Private residences

A gain on the disposal of a PPR is wholly exempt where the owner has occupied the whole residence throughout his period of ownership.

Where occupation has been for only part of a period, the proportion of the gain exempted is

$$\text{Total gain} \times \frac{\text{Period of occupation}}{\text{Total period of ownership}}$$

Periods of deemed occupation

- Absences of up to 3 years for any reason
- Absences while employed abroad
- Absences of up to 4 years while working elsewhere

These periods must normally be preceded and followed by a period of actual occupation

- Provided that there is no other main residence at the time.

Assessment focus

Draw up a table of exempt months and chargeable months. Check that the total of exempt and chargeable months is correct, to avoid making mistakes.

The last 36 months of ownership of a residence is always treated as a period of deemed occupation.

9: Shares

Topic List

The matching rules for shares and securities are extremely important. If you do not know the matching rules you will not be able to compute a gain on the disposal of shares.

You also need to be able to deal with bonus and rights issues.

Matching rules

Disposals by individual shareholders are matched with acquisitions in the following order:

- Same day acquisitions
- Acquisitions within the following 30 days (FIFO)
- Share pool

Assessment focus

Learn the 'matching rules' because a crucial first step to getting a shares question right is to correctly match the shares sold to the original shares purchased.

The share pool is kept in 2 columns:

(**1**) The **number** of shares

(**2**) The **cost**

Add the cost of any shares acquired to the cost column, or deduct a pro-rata slice from the cost column in respect of any shares disposed of.

When a company issues bonus shares all that happens is the size of the original holding is increased. The difference between a bonus issue and a rights issue is that in a rights issue the new shares are paid for.

Bonus issues

① Bonus issues relating to the share pool go into that pool.

② Simply add the number of shares to the pool: there is no cost.

Rights issues taken up

Rights issues relating to share pool are added to the number of shares and cost.

Notes

Notes

Notes

Notes

Notes

Notes